JOBS IN THE ARMY

by Emma Huddleston

Minneapolis, Minnesota

Credits
Cover and title page, © Chip Somodevilla/Getty Images, © TebNad/iStock, and © Denniro/iStock; 5T, © Cpl. Joseph Prado/DVIDS; 5B, © Gerhard Seuffert/DVIDS; 6–7, © Emanuel Leutze /Doe Memorial Library; 9, © Spc. Christian Carrillo/U. S. Army; 10, © Sgt. Emely Opio-Wright/DVIDS; 11T, © Operation 2022/Alamy Stock Photo; 11B, © Operation 2021/Alamy Stock Photo; 13T, © Army Sgt. Lianne Hirano/U. S. Department of Defense; 13B, © Barbara Romano/DVIDS; 14, © Maj. Jason Elmore/U. S. Army; 15, © SSgt Russ Jackson/Wikimedia Commons; 17T, © MUSTAFA TAUSEEF/Getty Images; 17B, © Jetlinerimages/iStock; 18–19, © Sgt. Justin Geiger/DVIDS; 21T, © Army Staff Sgt. Starla Lewis/U. S. Deparment of Defense; 21B, © Utilitiesman 3rd Class Christian Kinney/DVIDS; 23, © Chung Il Kim/DVIDS; 25, © C.J. Lovelace/DVIDS; 27T, © Cynthia McIntyre/DVIDS; 27B, © Staff Sgt. Shawn Morris/DVIDS; 28, © Stubby: Terrier Hero of Georgetown/Wikimedia Commons; 29, © Gertrud Zach/DVIDS, © Militarist/Shutterstock, © SHARKY PHOTOGRAPHY/Adobe Stock, and © Dontstop/iStock.

Bearport Publishing Company Product Development Team
President: Jen Jenson; Director of Product Development: Spencer Brinker; Managing Editor: Allison Juda; Associate Editor: Naomi Reich; Associate Editor: Tiana Tran; Art Director: Colin O'Dea; Designer: Kim Jones; Designer: Kayla Eggert; Product Development Assistant: Owen Hamlin

Statement on Usage of Generative Artificial Intelligence
Bearport Publishing remains committed to publishing high-quality nonfiction books. Therefore, we restrict the use of generative AI to ensure accuracy of all text and visual components pertaining to a book's subject. See BearportPublishing.com for details.

Library of Congress Cataloging-in-Publication Data

Names: Huddleston, Emma, author.
Title: Jobs in the Army / by Emma Huddleston.
Description: Minneapolis, Minnesota : Bearport Publishing Company, [2025] | Series: Military careers | Includes bibliographical references and index.
Identifiers: LCCN 2023059673 (print) | LCCN 2023059674 (ebook) | ISBN 9798892320351 (library binding) | ISBN 9798892321686 (ebook)
Subjects: LCSH: United States. Army--Vocational guidance--Juvenile literature.
Classification: LCC UB323 .H84 2025 (print) | LCC UB323 (ebook) | DDC 355.0023/73--dc23/eng/20240102
LC record available at https://lccn.loc.gov/2023059673
LC ebook record available at https://lccn.loc.gov/2023059674

Copyright © 2025 Bearport Publishing Company. All rights reserved. No part of this publication may be reproduced in whole or in part, stored in any retrieval system, or transmitted in any form or by any means, electronic, mechanical, photocopying, recording, or otherwise, without written permission from the publisher. Bearport Publishing is a division of Chrysalis Education Group.

For more information, write to Bearport Publishing, 5357 Penn Avenue South, Minneapolis, MN 55419.

CONTENTS

Safety in the Sky **4**
A Long History **6**
Beginning an Army Career **8**
Jobs on the Front Lines **12**
Intelligence Experts **16**
Builders of the Army **20**
Doctors on a Mission **22**
Jobs behind the Scenes **24**
Many Jobs for Soldiers **26**

More about the Army 28
Glossary 30
Read More 31
Learn More Online 31
Index 32
About the Author 32

SAFETY IN THE SKY

U.S. Army soldiers clutch their parachute packs as the plane's door opens. The wind rushes in, and one by one the soldiers jump into the empty sky below. Who makes sure these individuals stay safe?

Parachute riggers are special soldiers whose job is to pack and **inspect** parachutes before **missions**. They test the equipment, make necessary repairs, and ensure that all supplies are ready for each airdrop operation. This is just one of the many important jobs in the United States Army.

CAREER SPOTLIGHT: Parachute Rigger

Job Requirements:
- Entry level
- 16 weeks advanced training
- Active duty

Skills and Training:
 Rigging Supplies
 Testing and Inspection
 Maintenance and Repairs

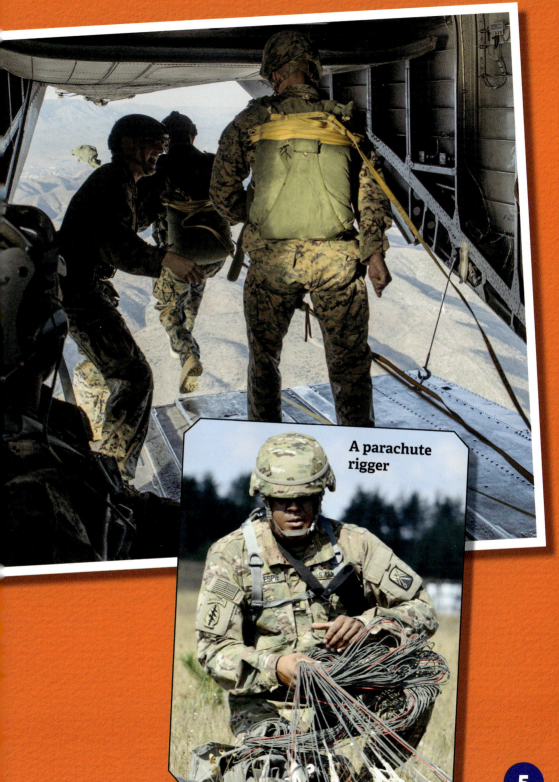

A parachute rigger

5

A LONG HISTORY

There has been an army in the United States since before the country officially formed! In 1775, American colonists were unhappy with the laws put in place by their British rulers. Members from all 13 colonies joined together to fight the British in the Revolutionary War (1775–1783). This army won freedom for an independent United States.

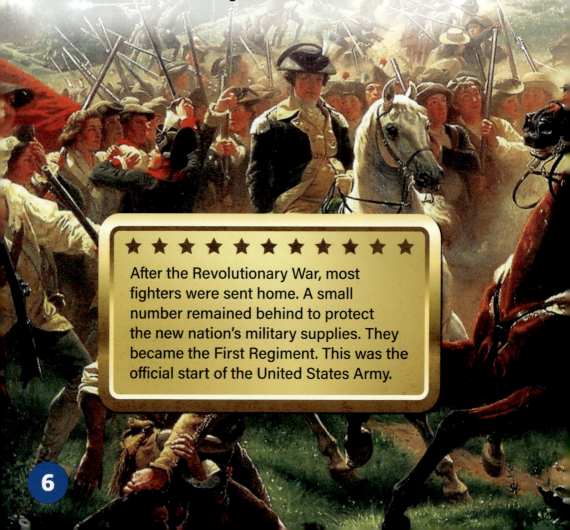

After the Revolutionary War, most fighters were sent home. A small number remained behind to protect the new nation's military supplies. They became the First Regiment. This was the official start of the United States Army.

Since this first war hundreds of years ago, the United States Army has participated in battles **abroad** and defended citizens stateside. Its goal has remained the same: to protect the United States and its people.

The Revolutionary War

BEGINNING AN ARMY CAREER

For **enlisted** soldiers, the first step toward a career in the army is to go through basic training, or boot camp. This intense 10-week training includes lessons in the classroom, where **recruits** learn about first aid, navigation, and army rules.

A large part of basic training is focused on getting in shape. Every morning of boot camp begins with 90 minutes of physical training. Recruits also face obstacle courses, diving behind walls, crawling under wires, and carrying one another. They train with weapons and learn different styles of **combat**.

★ ★ ★ ★ ★ ★ ★ ★ ★

Most members of the army are enlisted soldiers. This means they hold a **rank** lower than that of officers. Army officers get special training to lead soldiers in boot camp and beyond.

Army recruits practice rappelling down towers, using ropes to climb down walls quickly.

Near the end of boot camp, the soon-to-be soldiers must complete several final challenges. One is a **simulated** combat experience. The recruits practice what it would be like to hold off enemy forces. The most intense challenge lasts 81 hours. It involves traveling 40 miles (64 km) on foot while carrying heavy packs and gear. Recruits may hike as far as 10 miles (16 km), crawl through muck, and practice their gun skills all in a single day.

After 10 hard weeks, the soldiers take an **oath** to officially join the United States Army. Most go on to do more job-specific training from there.

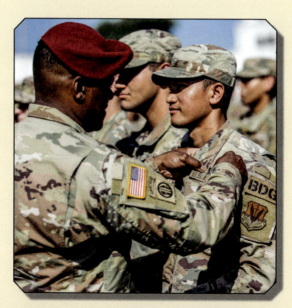

Recruits officially become soldiers when they finish basic training.

Many challenges during boot camp involve working as a team.

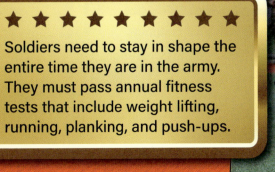

★ ★ ★ ★ ★ ★ ★ ★

Soldiers need to stay in shape the entire time they are in the army. They must pass annual fitness tests that include weight lifting, running, planking, and push-ups.

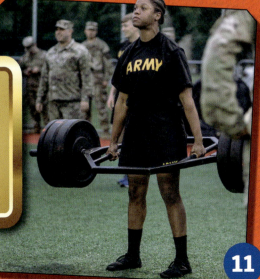

11

JOBS ON THE FRONT LINES

Some soldiers train for combat jobs that put them in battle zones. Infantrymen make up most of the troops on the ground at the front lines. These soldiers are sent out in the **field** around the world to fight enemy forces.

Field **artillery** officers lead some infantrymen on their missions. The officers with this job are defense experts, deciding which **tactics** to use during battle. They are in charge of choosing when and how to use large weapons, including cannons, rockets, and missiles.

CAREER SPOTLIGHT: Infantryman

Job Requirements:
- 17 to 34 years old
- 22 weeks basic and advanced training
- Active duty or national guard

Skills and Training:
- Weapons Operations
- Vehicle Operations
- Physical & Mental Strength

In addition to ground forces, the army has air teams on the front lines. Some fly in to drop supplies to soldiers below to help make sure infantrymen have what they need in battle.

For the most extreme missions, the army sends in **special operations forces** from the air. Night Stalkers are experts in the most advanced aircraft, and they fly to and from their dangerous missions under the cover of darkness. Their training includes learning how to use advanced fighting skills and weapons.

In addition to planes flown by soldiers in the aircraft, the army also uses drones. Drones are flown into especially dangerous missions. They can be controlled from a safe distance away.

Night Stalkers need to move quickly. They sometimes drop from helicopters directly behind enemy lines.

15

INTELLIGENCE EXPERTS

Military **intelligence** soldiers are responsible for gathering information that can help officers shape their strategies in the field. A geospatial intelligence imagery analyst works with information gathered from afar. They look at maps, **aerial** photos, videos, and other clues to gain knowledge about enemy locations. These soldiers may identify battle zones or obstacles that could prevent infantrymen from reaching their targets. They also search for weapons or aircraft bases that may be hiding enemy supplies.

CAREER SPOTLIGHT: Geospatial Intelligence Imagery Analyst

Job Requirements:
- 17 to 34 years old
- 22 weeks advanced training
- Active duty, reserve, or national guard

Skills and Training:
- Geospatial Analysis
- Identification & Strategy
- Electronic Monitoring

17

Calvary scouts are a special type of military intelligence soldier. They are the eyes and ears of the army. Their difficult job is to gather enemy intelligence from the ground without getting caught.

CAREER SPOTLIGHT: Calvary Scout

Job Requirements:
- 17 to 34 years old
- 22 weeks basic and advanced training
- Active duty or national guard

Skills and Training:
- Tracking & Reporting
- Weapons Operations
- Routes & Navigation

Calvary scouts use their **specialized** skills to learn where enemy forces are located and what they may be doing. These soldiers secretly gather information on enemy vehicles and weapons. They pass what they learn along to officers who can use it during the fighting.

BUILDERS OF THE ARMY

Army engineers are responsible for building, fixing, and maintaining the machines and technology of the military. Soldiers with this job have additional training after boot camp to develop skills in a specific type of engineering. Electrical engineers need to know how to install and maintain electrical systems for equipment and buildings.

The army's mechanical engineers can specialize in vehicles, boats, aircraft, or construction equipment. Within the aircraft specialties, some jobs require even more specific skills. Some aircraft engineers repair massive planes. Others work on small helicopters and drones.

> ★ ★ ★ ★ ★ ★ ★ ★ ★ ★ ★ ★ ★
>
> A carpentry and masonry specialist is another type of engineer in the army. This type of soldier builds with wood, concrete, stones, and bricks. The specialist constructs buildings and teaches combat soldiers how to make structures in the field.

DOCTORS ON A MISSION

Just like **civilians**, soldiers need help taking care of their health. The army has its own network of dentists, doctors, nurses, and surgeons that care for soldiers. These medical personnel are found everywhere from bases stateside to dangerous combat zones around the world.

In the field, battle wounds often need immediate attention, but providing medical aid can be difficult. Field surgeons are trained to work in areas with active fighting. In some cases, army surgeons even have to operate in moving aircraft.

CAREER SPOTLIGHT: Field Surgeon

Job Requirements:
- 21 to 42 years old
- Officer
- Active duty, reserve, or national guard

Skills and Training:
- Emergency Medical Care
- Patient Care
- Inspection & Sterilization

JOBS BEHIND THE SCENES

With hundreds of thousands of soldiers around the world, keeping track of people and supplies takes skilled workers. Automated logistical specialists are responsible for keeping track of supplies and equipment. They maintain records of items coming and going from warehouses. Once things get to the troops, unit supply specialists unload, store, and distribute the items. Soldiers in these important roles help make sure others get what they need to do their jobs.

CAREER SPOTLIGHT: Automated Logistical Specialist

Job Requirements:
- 17 to 34 years old
- 12 weeks advanced training
- Active duty, reserve, or national guard

Skills and Training:
- Record Keeping
- Data Analysis
- Stocking & Storage

MANY JOBS FOR SOLDIERS

Some jobs in the army are a lot like those in civilian life. Army musicians play during ceremonies and to entertain their fellow soldiers. Firefighter soldiers work to prevent fires. They fight the flames and rescue their fellow soldiers if a fire does break out. Chaplains lead religious services and put on special events for soldiers and their families.

From troops on the ground to those who work on operations behind the scenes, the army is full of soldiers with many different careers. Together, they help keep the army ready to protect the country.

Many people in the army are active duty. They work for the military full-time. Some, however, are part-time. Soldiers in the army reserve or national guard often have civilian jobs, too.

Army firefighters work on military bases as well as aboard ships and aircraft.

MORE ABOUT THE ARMY

AT A GLANCE

Founded: June 14, 1775
Membership: More than 400,000
Categories of ranks: Enlisted soldier, warrant officer, and commissioned officer
Largest base: Fort Liberty in North Carolina

DID YOU KNOW?

- George Washington was the first commander in chief of the army. Later, he became the first president of the United States.

- In today's army, a single infantryman may have to carry more than 100 pounds (45 kg) of gear at a time.

- Famous singer Elvis Presley joined the United States Army during the late 1950s. He served in Germany.

- A dog named Stubby joined the 26th Division of the United States Army during World War I (1914–1918). Stubby was the only dog to be promoted to the rank of sergeant through combat.

Stubby

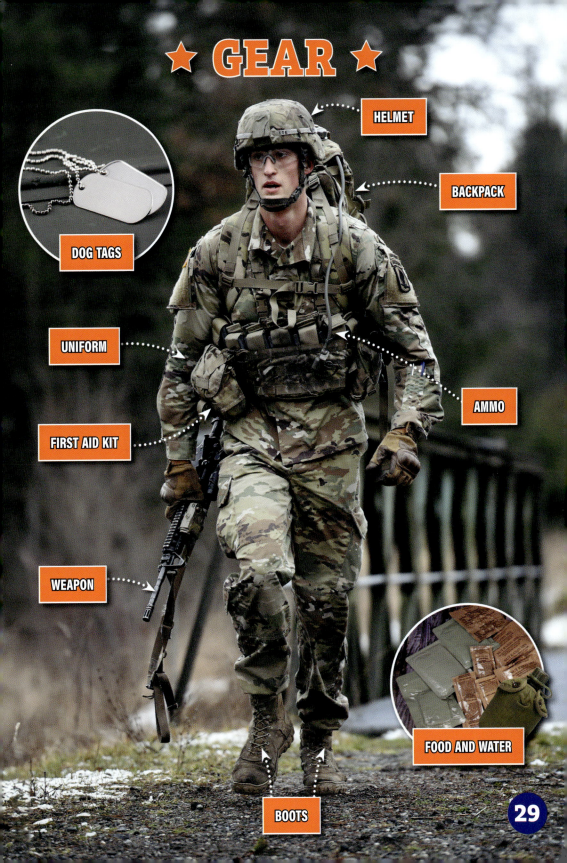

GLOSSARY

abroad in a foreign country

aerial from the sky

artillery large guns that shoot over long distances

civilians people who are not in the military

combat fighting or having to do with fighting between people or armies

enlisted soldiers who have joined a branch of the armed forces without prior special training and hold a rank below officer

field in the military, a place where a battle is fought

inspect to check details closely

intelligence in war, information about a possible enemy or area

missions tasks that have a particular goal

oath a promise to be faithful to a body, organization, or country

rank an official position or level in the military

recruits people who are going through the process of joining the army

simulated made to look or feel real

specialized focused on one subject or area of work

special operations forces a branch of the United States Army made up of soldiers specially trained in intense, on-the-ground warfare

tactics ways of doing things to win a battle

READ MORE

Morey, Allan. *U.S. Army (U.S. Armed Forces)*. Minneapolis: Jump!, 2021.

Noll, Elizabeth. *Armor (Military Science)*. Minneapolis: Bellwether Media, 2022.

Ventura, Marne. *U.S. Army (U.S. Armed Forces)*. Minneapolis: Kaleidoscope, 2023.

LEARN MORE ONLINE

1. Go to **www.factsurfer.com** or scan the QR code below.

2. Enter "**Army Jobs**" into the search box.

3. Click on the cover of this book to see a list of websites.

INDEX

aircraft 14, 16, 20, 22, 27
basic training 8, 10, 12, 18
calvary scout 18–19
chaplain 26
combat 8, 10, 12, 20, 22, 28
doctor 22
engineer 20
enlisted soldier 8, 28
firefighter 26–27
field artillery officer 12
infantryman 12, 14, 16, 28
intelligence 16, 18
musician 26
missions 4, 12, 14, 22
Night Stalker 14–15
officer 8, 12, 16, 19, 22, 28
parachute rigger 4–5
recruits 8–10
Revolutionary War 6–7
supplies 4, 6, 14, 16, 24
vehicles 12, 19–20

ABOUT THE AUTHOR

Emma Huddleston lives with her family in the Twin Cities. She enjoys reading, taking walks, and swing dancing. To all those who serve in the military, she says thank you!